# Track Changes

## EASY WORD ESSENTIALS 2019

## BOOK 5

## M.L. HUMPHREY

# SELECT TITLES BY M.L. HUMPHREY

## WORD ESSENTIALS 2019

Word 2019 Beginner

Word 2019 Intermediate


## EASY WORD ESSENTIALS 2019

Text Formatting

Page Formatting

Lists

Tables

Track Changes

# CONTENTS

# Introduction

The *Easy Word Essentials 2019* series of books is designed for those users who just want to learn one specific topic rather than have a more general introduction to Microsoft Word 2019, which is provided in *Word 2019 Beginner* and *Word 2019 Intermediate*.

Each book in this series covers one specific topic such as formatting, tables, or track changes.

I'm going to assume in these books that you have a basic understanding of Microsoft Word. However, this book does include an appendix with basic terminology just in case I use a term that isn't familiar to you or that isn't used the way you're used to.

This entire series of books is written for users of Word 2019. If you have a different version of Word then you might want to read the *Easy Word Essentials* series instead which is written as a more general approach to learning Microsoft Word.

For most introductory topics there won't be much of a difference between the two, but just be aware that this particular series does not worry about compatibility with other versions of Word whereas the more general series does.

Also, just a reminder that the content of this book is directly pulled from *Word 2019 Beginner* and/or *Word 2019 Intermediate* so there may be references in the text that indicate that.

Alright. Now that the preliminaries are out of the way, let's dive in with a discussion of track changes and comparing documents.

# Compare Two Documents

Track Changes is a complex one, so I thought I'd cover something related first and that's how to compare two documents.

I have needed this multiple times in my career. One of the big ones is when someone goes through a document I've sent them and makes edits but they don't use track changes and I have no idea what has been changed.

With the type of work I've done in the past a single changed comma can be significant, so to make sure I catch and review every single change I will compare the document they sent back to the document I sent them.

What comparing documents does is it creates a new document that takes the first document and notes all changes on it that would have led to the second document. Every deletion, insertion, format change, etc. is marked.

It basically creates a version that looks like track changes was used.

To do this, first, be sure that both documents you want to use have been saved. Word won't compare unsaved documents.

Next, open any document in Word. It can be one of the documents you want to use, but Word will make you find the documents you want to compare anyway, so it doesn't have to be. The key is to have Word open so you can access the Review tab.

Go to the Review tab and click on the dropdown under the Compare section and choose the Compare option. (We're not going to discuss Combine here. My super-attentive-to-detail self refuses to use it. There are just too many ways for a combine option to go wrong for me to trust it.)

When you choose the compare option, you will see the Compare Documents dialogue box.

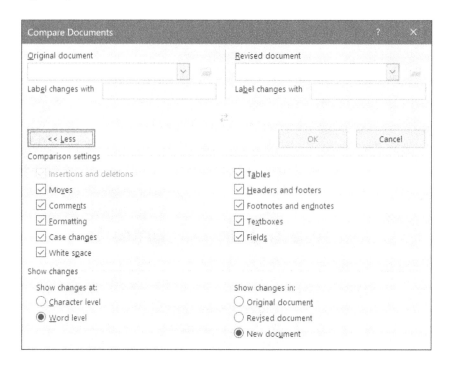

I've clicked on the More button here to show you all of the options available. The default view just shows you the two dropdown menus where you choose which document to treat as the original and which to treat as the new document.

Next to each of the dropdown menus is a small folder image.

You can either see if the documents you need are in the dropdown or you can use the folder image to bring up a dialogue box that lets you navigate to where you have the document saved.

Which document you list as the original and which you list as the revised document matters because Word will mark changes based upon what has been done to the document you identify as the original.

For example, take the following sentence:

"What are you doing here, Carl?"

Let's say the name was wrong and should've been Bob, so the person editing the document changed it. If you compare the documents in the correct order you should see a line through Carl and then Bob as the replacement text. If you compare them in the wrong order, though, it will look like Bob was replaced with Carl.

So always be careful to select the correct original document and correct revised document.

Once you select both documents, Word will list a name under the Revised Document to show who will be listed as the author of any edits. I usually have to change this, because I want the changes labeled with the name of the person who sent me the document, not my name.

In the More section you have additional options to choose what changes are identified.

I never mess with the default settings on compare, they all work fine for me, although there have probably been times I could've turned off tracking formatting changes and been much happier since I visually inspect for formatting issues.

Once you've made all of your choices, click on OK and Word will do the comparison.

If you've left the other settings untouched, this will be done in a new document. You result will look something like this:

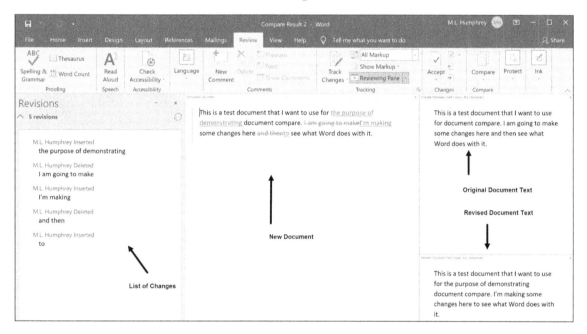

On the left-hand side will be a listing of each change that was made between the two documents.

In the center will be the new document that was created using track changes. Inserted text is red and underlined. Deleted text is read and has a strikethrough. (See the section on track changes for a longer discussion on how this works.)

On the right-hand side the text in both the original and revised documents is shown.

This makes it very easy to walk through and see what the original had, what was changed, and what the revised document looks like.

Keep in mind that sometimes Word labels things as changes that really aren't. For example, I just ran Compare on a paperback I had recently reformatted and it shows font changes that I hadn't technically made to the document. What I had done is accidentally deleted a header or two and had to retype the text. Even though I didn't change the font, Word labeled that as a font change.

Compare also doesn't do well if large chunks of text have been added or moved around.

I've seen it miss that a paragraph of text was inserted from later in the document and then flag everything from that point forward as a change even though it really wasn't.

(If that ever happens to you, I'd recommend creating a middle version of the document where you just move the blocks of text but don't have the edits yet and then running Compare on that interim document. That way you still get to see the smaller changes that were made.)

Basically, it's a useful tool, but it's not perfect.

I should also add that I don't think I've ever had a situation where Compare failed to identify a change. When it errs it errs on the side of identifying more changes than there actually were.

Okay, time to talk about track changes so that you know how to look at the changes Compare flagged between your two documents and so that hopefully you just never need to use it because track changes were used up front.

# Track Changes

I love track changes. It is a fantastic tool and I'm not sure how I lived without it before it existed. You can write a document, give it to a group for review, they can make their changes in track changes, and you can easily see what they did. It's wonderful.

But...

I've been putting off writing this part of the book because track changes is also somewhat finicky. And it's changed with different versions of Word.

I know, for example, that copy and paste have pretty much stayed the same for the last twenty years. Not the case with track changes. This is probably one of the tools in Word that they like to mess with the most between releases. So the version of track changes you have in Word 2019 is not the same as in any other version of Word and it is probably the tool most likely to change in the next version of Word.

But the basics remain the same. So let's see what we can cover.

## Overview

What is track changes?

It's a way for you to see what changes have been made in a document and by whom they were made and when they were made. (So no telling your boss you were working late editing that document when you weren't. One little look at track changes will show you were actually done by four.)

I have had issues in the past when using track changes with tables or formatting changes because the changes either weren't marked appropriately or the ultimate document didn't look the way it appeared it would when track changes were on. More recent versions of Word probably don't have this issue as much, but it's something to be aware of.

This is why I strongly recommend that when you think your document is final, you accept all changes in your document, and then read that document from first page to last. Do not just accept all changes in a document and be done. You need to do one final review of that document to make sure that everything looks the way it should. You don't want to miss something weird like a double period that is only noticeable when the changes have been accepted.

Some of this you can see with different view options, but still. Save all changes and review a clean copy.

AND, this one is huge, be sure that track changes are turned off in your final document and that you've inspected the document to remove all tracked changes and comments.

I have on occasion as both a consultant and regulator been given a document by a client or someone I was investigating that still included track changes or comments. They were turned off, but they were not removed and all it took was one little click to turn them back on and see the interesting discussion about how to phrase something problematic.

Not good. At best something like that just looks sloppy. At worst it could lose you a law suit.

So track changes are great, but know how to use them and how to finalize a document if you do use them.

Okay.

## Getting Started

I never turn on track changes until the first draft of my document has been written. It should be obvious to everyone that the base text was a draft and I don't need the entire document to be underlined in red.

Once I'm ready to review a document that's been provided to me for review or to circulate a document for review by others, that's the time to turn on track changes.

To do so, go to the Tracking section of the Review tab, click on the arrow under Track Changes, and choose Track Changes from the dropdown.

This will turn on track changes in your document but nothing will happen until you then make an edit to the document. Assuming you're in full markup view, text you delete will be shown with a strikethrough and text you add will be underlined. Both will be color-coded based upon who made the edit. Each user is assigned a specific color with the first person who made edits usually assigned red, the second blue, and so on and so on.

If you ever need to turn off track changes, you can simply click on that option again in the Tracking section or right-click on a tracked change in your document and click on Track Changes from the dropdown menu.

Either option will turn off track changes for any *new* edits to the document, but it will not remove already tracked changes. Those need to be accepted or rejected.

## Track Changes Notation

Here is a sample of text where I've added and deleted some words:

> This is a sample sentence that I ~~want to edit~~have edited so that you can see how t~~T~~rack c~~C~~hanges works.

The original text read "This is a sample sentence that I want to edit so that you can see how Track Changes works."

I then changed it to read "This is a sample sentence that I have edited so that you can see how track changes works."

The phrase "want to edit" is struck through because it was deleted. The phrase that replaced it "have edited" is underlined because it was added.

Also, the T and C in Track Changes are struck through because they were deleted and replaced with a lower case t and c which are underlined.

(Sometimes, at least in past versions of track changes, Word will show the whole word as edited, not just the one letter, but that could be more when working with document compare than directly in track changes.)

If you look to the left of the line you'll see a gray mark. This indicates that there is a change in that line or at that point in the document.

It's simple enough to see the changes in the example above, but if the change is a deleted or added comma it can be easy to miss. That little mark off to the side is a quick way to scan a page to find if any changes were made on the page.

Another way to do so is to use the Previous and Next options that are available in the Changes section of the Review tab.

Clicking on either of those options will move through your document one change at a time.

As you move through the document, each change will be highlighted in gray.

While Next and Previous are a great way to not miss a single change in your document, sometimes it can be absurdly annoying to use them because literally every change is treated separately.

In the example above where at a glance I can see that Track Changes was replaced with track changes, using Next on those changes would mean four separate stops, one for the deletion of each of the capital letters and one for the insertion of their lower case replacements.

In those situations, if I'm accepting or rejecting changes as I go (which I tend not to do), I'd highlight both words and accept all four changes at once.

Speaking of accepting or rejecting changes, let's cover that now.

## Accept or Reject Changes

Track changes will note all the changes you make in your document while it's turned on. But to finalize your document, you ultimately need to accept or reject every change you've made.

My preferred method of doing this is to read through the entire document and make sure I agree with all of the changes and then accept all changes in the document at once.

To do that, go to the Changes section of the Review tab, click on the arrow under Accept, and choose Accept All Changes or Accept All Changes and Stop Tracking.

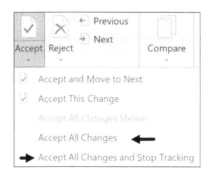

Which choice you make really depends on who has control of the document at that point and what could happen from that point forward. My personal preference is to not accept the changes until I'm also ready to stop tracking.

But I've also had situations with a team where someone made a problematic last-minute change and no one else knew about it because track changes had already been turned off.

So...Both options have their uses.

In the same way that you can accept all changes in a document at once you can also reject all changes in a document at once using the Reject dropdown menu. (Why you'd go to all that effort and then reject them, I don't know, but it's an option that exists.)

Where I do use the Reject dropdown is for the other choices, Reject and Move To Next or Reject Change:

You can use the Accept and Move to Next and Reject and Move to Next options to move through every change in your document and accept or reject them as you go.

If you accept a change, Word will turn added text to normal text or delete deleted text. If you reject a change, Word will put deleted text back as normal text and delete any added text.

The reason I generally don't take this approach is two-fold. First, because it makes it look like there was no change made, which is not ideal when working in teams.

Say, for example, I'm on a project with five people and I'm supposed to review that document third. I believe the person reviewing it fourth or fifth has the right to see the original document and the edits made by each reviewer. The only way for that to happen is for me to not accept or reject changes.

(Often this is where Comments, which we'll talk about next, can be useful. One person says X, I disagree and type in an edit and then add a comment off to the side to explain why I've disagreed and made that edit, especially if the edit erased a change.)

I think the key in determining whether to edit over an edit or to accept/reject comes down to the nature of the edit. If it's just deleting an extra period or adding a period at the end of a paragraph, who cares? Accept, Reject, fine. Other changes require more consideration than that.

The second reason I tend not to accept or reject changes as I go is that it many changes are paired changes. I deleted X and replaced it with Y. But when walking through a document and accepting/rejecting changes one at a time those changes are split into two separate changes that need to be reviewed and accepted or rejected individually.

(One way around this is to select an entire word or sentence and choose Accept This Change which should accept all changes in that selection.)

For individual changes, you can also right-click directly on a tracked change in your document to accept or reject that change using the dropdown menu.

## Reviewing Changes

In the sample I showed above it isn't immediately obvious who made the change or when they made it but there are ways to see that, so let's walk through those now.

### *Users and Time*

One quick way to see who made a change as well as a description of the change is to hold your mouse over each change. When you do that a little box will appear with the user name, time, type of change, and text changed. Like so:

M.L. Humphrey, 1/16/2021 2:16:00 PM
inserted:
have edited

have edited so that you can

I put my mouse over the text "have edited" and a little comment box appears to show that M.L. Humphrey made that edit on 1/16/2021 at 2:16 PM, that the text was inserted, and that what was inserted was "have edited".

Usually you're not going to do this for every edit. But when you have multiple users on a document it can be a quick way to see which user a color represents. I'll probably hover over each color once to get it into my head which color belongs to which user as I start reviewing the document.

(You need to do this each time, because the color assigned to each user is not fixed. I can be red in one document and blue in the next.)

To easily see who made each edit without holding your mouse over the comment and to also see the full text of any comments, use a reviewing pane.

## *Reviewing Panes (Revision Pane)*

To turn on a reviewing pane, go to the Tracking section of the Review tab and click on Reviewing Pane or the arrow next to it to see the dropdown menu.

By default clicking on Reviewing Pane will open a Revisions pane off to the left side of the main workspace. Using the dropdown menu you can instead choose Reviewing Pane Horizontal to open a Revisions pane below the workspace.

The Revisions pane lists out the user name, type of change, and change for each change made in the document as well as the full text of all comments made in the document. Here is an example of a vertical pane:

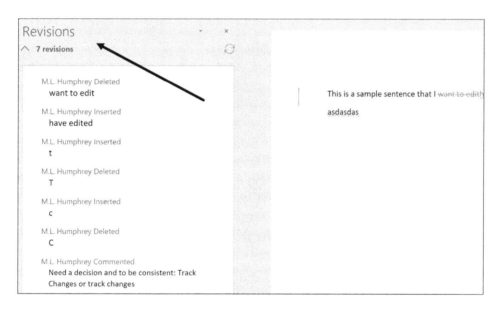

This is another useful way to make sure that you catch each and every change in the document. It's also helpful when working with documents that have extensive comments in them.

It is especially helpful if you have the track change view of your document set to not actually show the changes in the document itself. (A view that I personally DO NOT like, but that seems to be the default these days.)

To close the Reviewing Pane you can click on the option again or click on the X in the top right corner of the pane itself.

# Track Changes Views

There are four possible choices for viewing track changes in your document, Simple Markup, All Markup, No Markup, and Original. Each can be accessed through the top dropdown menu on the right side of the Tracking section of the Review tab.

Let's walk through all four.

## *All Markup*

This is a sample sentence that I ~~want to edit~~<u>have edited</u> so that you can see how t~~T~~rack c~~C~~hanges works.

This is the one I prefer because it shows both what's been deleted and what's been added. You can see the strikethrough of the deleted text and the underline of the added text as we discussed previously

## *Simple Markup*

This is a sample sentence that I have edited so that you can see how track changes works.

Simple markup shows the document text in final form but indicates that there was a change made at that point in the document by using a bright red line off to the left side. It also will show any comments that were made.

## *No Markup*

No Markup shows the document text in final form *with no indication that changes have been made in the document*. It also does not show comments.

This in my opinion is the most dangerous view because this is the one where you forget that track changes are actually still turned on, which as I mentioned before can be very problematic under certain circumstances.

This view can have its uses like seeing what the final document will look like with all changes incorporated. But I would highly, highly recommend that you never leave your document in this view. Use it and immediately change it back.

And if you work with someone who uses this view, be sure to always check any document they give you before you send it on as a final document to make sure that track changes have in fact been turned off, all comments have been deleted, and all changes in the document have actually been accepted.

### *Original*

Original shows the document as it was before any changes were made. This can be convenient to toggle on briefly when there are a lot of changes in a section of a document to see what the original text was, but as with No Markup it would be a very bad idea to leave this view on because you would not see that there are tracked changes in the document.

If you then accepted all changes, you'd be accepting changes to the document you didn't realize existed.

I'd recommend before you start reviewing any document that you check the view it is in. (Nothing worse than getting halfway through a document, being furious at someone for not having caught all the issues you are, and then realizing they did catch them but you couldn't see it because the document was in Original view.)

## Show Markup Dropdown

You can also choose the type of changes you want to see in your document using the Show Markup dropdown menu in the Tracking section of the Review tab.

In Word 2019 the default is to have Comments, Insertions and Deletions, and Formatting visible, but you can click on any of those options to remove them from your view. (I will often in a complex document turn off formatting.)

If one of those options is already turned off, you can click on it to show that type of change.

The Balloons option works with the full markup view. I generally leave this one as is with comments and formatting changes noted off to the side. That looks like this:

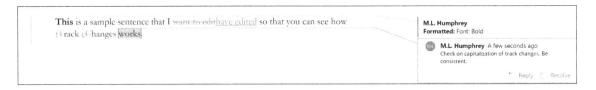

Show Revisions in Balloons shows the final version of the text with insertions still marked but the deletions listed off to the side. Like so:

Show All Revisions In Line will not have anything noted off to the side. Formatting only shows if you hold your mouse over the formatted text to see the note. A comment will show as the user's initials in brackets along with the number of the comment [MH1]. You can see the actual comment by holding your mouse over the initials. (Not my preferred view.)

## Changes By Multiple Users

As mentioned before, unless something is off about the settings on your document, each individual user who makes changes to the document will be assigned a different color for their changes. When it's just one person making edits to the document using track changes, those changes are generally shown in red. The next user is in blue, etc., etc.

This isn't based on who the user is, so you can be assigned the color red in one document and green in another. If you hold your mouse over any specific change, Word will tell you who the user was who made the changes and when they made them.

(If your document has been stripped of personalization, it's possible to have all changes in the document show up under Author and to not be able to tell who made what change. I would highly recommend that you do not strip personalization from a document that you intend to continue working on.)

If for some reason someone hasn't customized their version of Word (which is rare in corporate settings and probably impossible in newer versions of Word) the changes they make will also show up as Author. If you happen to have two users who have done this, their changes will be combined under the same color and user name and you won't be able to tell them apart.

The dropdown under Show Markup will let you see just the changes made by one user by going to the Specific People option and then unchecking user names. If you have a lot of reviewers for a document, click on All Reviewers to turn off all tracked changes for all users and then go back to click on the user you want to see.

(I don't think I've ever actually reviewed a document one user at a time, but you can. If you ever feel tempted to do so, maybe stop and ask why because that points to a team dynamic issue for me. At the end of the day the whole document has to work together regardless of who made what change. But as I think about this more, maybe if I hired an editor and wanted to see those edits but didn't want to see my own edits in response I could use this? Maybe...I don't know.)

## Track Changes With Tables, Lists, and Formatting

I tend to be a little leery about using track changes with tables. I just tried making a bunch of changes to a table in Word and it was okay, but it's still something I approach with care and prefer to do outside of track changes when I can.

For example, I added Shading to cells in my table and as far as I can tell, Word didn't note that as a change. It did capture new text I entered into my table cells. And it flagged an added row to the table in blue and a deleted row in pink. It also caught my bolding of text.

But what it tends to miss is any sort of design work on the table itself. I changed the width of two columns and the height of one row and Word treated all of that as one change that I could either reject or keep.

Also, in this case choosing to reject all changes on my table led to a very strange result. It did not return the table to its original format.

Which is all to say that I would still be wary of using track changes on tables in Word 2019 unless the only changes being made to the table were to the text in the cells in the table.

With lists the issue is looking at them in All Markup mode, because I can't see the indents properly.

If I've done anything to change the numbering, so if I swapped a list from 1, 2, 3 to A, B, C, for example, the way that that's tracked in All Markup can be hard to review.

One solution is to change the Show Markup option to Show Revisions in Balloons instead or while looking at the list to swap over to the No Markup or Simple Markup view.

Honestly, overall I would recommend that any big formatting happen without track changes on and that you try to limit your actions when track changes is turned on to text edits as much as possible. Your life will be simpler if you do it that way.

*  *  *

Okay. So that was track changes. A very useful tool for group work.

Now to cover something I've always used in connection with track changes, comments, which are actually separate because you can add comments to a document without ever turning on track changes.

Just remember two things before we move on: Always remember to accept/reject all changes in your document and to turn off track changes when you're done. And never, ever, ever use formatting of your text to replicate the appearance of track changes rather than actually using track changes.

# Comments

I often think of comments in conjunction with track changes because that's where they tend to be used the most.

For example, you make an edit in a document and want to say something about it to the others who are reviewing the document so put a comment off to the side. Or have a question about something someone said, so put the question in a comment.

But, actually, comments can be used separate from track changes. You can insert a comment into a document that has never had track changes turned on. And you *definitely* should use the comments function rather than add a comment or question into the text of a document where it doesn't belong. It's far easier to delete comments from a document than track down every bracketed [verify this] hidden in the text of a document.

I have actually seen people do all of the following with a comment added to the text of a document: highlight it, put it in brackets, underline it, bold it, and/or change the color of the text.

The only one of those that is easy to find is the bracketed version.

Maybe the highlight can be found easily without scrolling through every page of the document. But underlined? There might be legitimately underlined text in that document. Bolded? Same.

So do not do that. Do not do any of that.

(I will say this is probably me wasting my breath because when I've seen this happen it was generally by someone very senior who started their career back when there were secretaries whose sole job was to type up these people's hand-written notes. Which means the person who most needs to hear this is not reading this book)

Okay then. One final point before I move on. There is a time to use brackets in a document. Usually when information is still missing and needs to be filled in before the document can be finalized. Sometimes when I'm writing fiction I don't want to stop and research some minor detail so I'll set that off in brackets. Or you may do this with a class paper. For example, "The first shot fired in the Civil War occurred at [PLACE] on [DATE]."

(Also please, don't ever do what one of my MBA classmates did which was turn in his portion of a paper with [If I'd written this, this is what I would've actually discussed in this paragraph]. Not cool.)

Okay. Sorry about that tangent. Clearly I have had some bad experiences with misused commenting in documents.

Getting back to the point: When you have comments to insert into a Word document it is best to use the Comments feature.

To do so, click on a location in the document where you want your comment linked. (You cannot link a comment to a footnote, so if your comment relates to a footnote, link to either the point in the main text of the document where the footnote occurred or link to a point at the bottom of the page (my preference) that is near the actual text of the footnote.)

Next, go to the Comments section of the Review tab and click on New Comment. Word will usually highlight the nearest word and then link to a comment off to the right side of your text. The comment will have your name on it and you can then type whatever it is you need to say below that.

If you have Original or No Markup selected in the Track Changes section, inserting a comment will open the Revisions pane on the left-hand side of your document. You can type your comment in there just as easily. Click on any comment in that pane to see the word that it links to in the document.

When you're done entering your comment, click back into your document. (Enter will not work since that just adds a line break within the comment itself.)

If your comments are visible on the right-hand side of your document (so you're in Simple Markup or All Markup view), you can reply to an existing comment by clicking on the Reply option which will be visible when you hold your mouse over that comment.

Doing so will create a new sub-comment under the first comment that is labeled with your name. You can then type in whatever response you would like as I've done in this example.

If you are looking at comments using the Revisions pane, then to reply to a comment, you need to right-click on the comment and choose Reply to Comment from the dropdown menu.

The Revisions pane option will not show the relationship between the two comments the same way that viewing them via Simple Markup or All Markup on the right-hand side of the page does. The reply is just listed like a normal comment.

So if you have a conversation that is occurring via comments, I'd recommend using Simple Markup or All Markup.

Your other option for responding to a comment is to resolve it. On the right-hand side you can click on Resolve. In the Revisions pane you can right-click and choose Resolve Comment.

When you resolve a comment, on the right-hand side that comment will be grayed-out. In the Revisions pane there's really not a noticeable difference, but the highlight of the word the comment is linked to in the document will be a lighter shade of pink.

So again, the Simple Markup or All Markup view is the better view to use in this case.

If a comment has been marked as resolved, you can reopen it.

To move between comments, use the Previous and Next options in the Comments section of the Review tab.

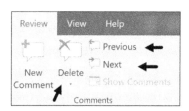

If a document is set to All Markup and Show All Revisions Inline then comments will appear as a set of initials and a number in brackets within the text of the document, like [MLH1]. You can hold your cursor over those initials to see the comment.

If you don't see comments in your document, but think there should be comments, use the Previous or Next option in the Comments section and they will appear.

I generally review comments in connection with track changes. If you do that, then use the Previous and Next options in the Changes section of the Review tab instead of the Previous and Next options in the Comments section because this will allow you to walk through all changes as well as all comments.

Also, since comments are treated separately from track changes, accepting all changes or rejecting all changes in a document and then turning off track changes *will not* remove the comments from the document. You must do that separately.

To remove comments, go to the Comments section of the Review tab and under the Delete option choose Delete All Comments In Document to delete all of the comments in the document.

You can also use the dropdown to delete a single comment by clicking on that comment and choosing Delete from the dropdown instead.

Deleted comments are not reflected in track changes, so be careful when deleting comments that that choice is appropriate. Marking a comment as resolved may be better until the entire team has finished their review.

Just like with track changes, if you used comments in your document at any point it is always a best practice to check that all comments have been deleted before finalizing the document.

# Conclusion

Alright, so that was the basics of track changes in Word 2019. If you get stuck, reach out and I'm happy to help if I can. I don't check email every day, but I do check it regularly.

Good luck with it.

And if you decide that you want to learn more about Microsoft Word or Word 2019, feel free to check out my other books.

# Appendix A: Basic Terminology

Below are some basic terms that I use throughout this guide.

## Tab

I refer to the menu choices at the top of the screen (File, Home, Insert, Design, Layout, References, Mailings, Review, View, and Help) as tabs.

## Click

If I tell you to click on something, that means to use your mouse (or trackpad) to move the arrow on the screen over to a specific location and left-click or right-click on the option. If I don't specify which to use, left-click.

## Select or Highlight

If I tell you to select text, that means to highlight that text either by using your mouse or the arrow and shift keys. Selected text is highlighted in gray.

## Dropdown Menu

A dropdown menu provides you a list of choices to select from. There are dropdown menus when you right-click in your document workspace as well as for some of the options listed under the tabs at the top of the screen. Each option with a small arrow next to it will have a dropdown menu available.

# Expansion Arrows

I refer to the little arrows at the bottom right corner of most of the sections in each tab as expansion arrows. For example, click on the expansion arrow in the Clipboard section of the Home tab and it will open the Clipboard task pane.

# Dialogue Box

Dialogue boxes are pop-up boxes that cover specialized settings. They allow the most granular level of control over an option.

# Scroll Bar

Scroll bars are on the right-hand side of the workspace and sometimes along the bottom. They allow you to scroll through your document if your text takes up more space than you can see in the workspace.

# Arrow

If I ever tell you to arrow to the left or right or up or down, that just means use your arrow keys.

# Task Pane

I refer to the panes that sometimes appear to the left, right, and bottom of the main workspace as task panes. By default you should see the Navigation task pane on the left-hand side when you open a new document in Word.

# Control Shortcut

I'll occasionally mention control shortcuts that you can use to perform tasks. When I reference them I'll do so by writing it as Ctrl + a capital letter. For example, Save is Ctrl + S.

To use one, hold down the Ctrl key and the letter at the same time.

# ABOUT THE AUTHOR

M.L. Humphrey is a former stockbroker with a degree in Economics from Stanford and an MBA from Wharton who has spent close to twenty years as a regulator and consultant in the financial services industry.

You can reach M.L. Humphrey at:

mlhumphreywriter@gmail.com

or at

www.mlhumphrey.com

www.ingramcontent.com/pod-product-compliance
Lightning Source LLC
Chambersburg PA
CBHW060513060326
40689CB00020B/4733